DOXIES AND BONES

A COLLECTION OF POEMS AND RUINS

DR. SHRENIK RAVINDRA JAIN

For mother and father.

You made me exist.

Contents

Contents

Foreword

Shrenik Jain is a budding and an aspiring poet. His collection of poems entitled "Doxies and Bones" which is coming in a book form is really a pleasing moment. Let me elaborate this statement. Since 1990s onwards, it has been observed that the stream of Indian English poetry has been drying. The major reason for this may lie in the internet revolution. With the boom of IT and the social media, there is a major blow for poetry publishing houses. No doubt, the bestselling novels and success literature has remained in high demand. But on the front of poetry (and to some extent drama) there is silence. Does it mean that the form of poetry is waning fast? No way. It's blooming and flourishing from all the sides – Facebook walls, personal blogs, dedicated websites and YouTube channels are the new platforms where one can see how predominantly and forcefully the poetry form is prevalent. But these new age platforms have their own limitations. If we ask who the good poets are writing in this space, we'll have to take a long pause. The reason is, mainly it's a virtual world; much of the so called 'good content' which was popular yesterday, is now unavailable in digital memory and in public memory too. Good poetry or for that matter any literary form can be determined in terms of its age. If that work of art survives passing the test of time, it has valid reason to consider it as a good work. So it's the dire need of time that some scholars, some agencies to come forward to edit the online literature and bring it in book form so that it could go to the larger audience and God willing, will be sustained for a longer time.

In that sense, Shrenik Jain's this collection of poems is really soothing news. His poems in this collection can be broadly divided into personal poems and social poems. Shrenik's personal poems are mainly the love themed poems where the beloved is gone and the lover while living along with her memories is hopeful to meet her once again. For unknown reasons, the speaker knows it well that it's not going to be a happy story— "this winter love/that was/born in fall/bound/to fail/let's never/look back/to this season/let's forget/this year and its/reasons" ("Winter"). The speaker goes on recalling the intense and joyful moments they have shared together. While exploring the joys of love, the lover wonders, "i wish that i had been/a pirate in previous years/captaining distant seas/plundering shores/of different dialects/primate in habitat/with primal tongues/that hadn't tasted nothing" ("H.e.r."). But with her departure, he is "haunted by her absence" and finds the life dull, boring and painful. He wants an escape from her torturing memories. Thus the poet conveys beautifully the intense and passionate feelings of love; the journey that begins with warmth and enthusiasm approaches ultimately towards the feeling of sadness and melancholy.

The strain of sadness and melancholy continues through the social poems too. The poem "Sayan" portrays the element of discrimination on the basis of colour and caste, and compels Sayan to accept that an isolated world is a safer world; and at the same, the speaker does not forget to warn him that "Summer is far away". The poem "Maslow's Pyramid" is a direct attack on Maslow's concept of the hierarchy of needs. In "The Window" the poet depicts the inside/outside dilemma as he finds chaotic, disordered world on both the sides. In "World War Next", the poet visualises the horrors of the post-apocalyptic time. Or in a poem like "R. V. Human" he poses a sarcastic rhetoric question (Are we human?) for which his answer is a big no, because he assumes that "unchained hands were never worthy of freedom".

While reading Shrenik Jain's poems, one thing becomes very clear that his writing is original, he is not writing under anyone's influence. His poetry is not a region specific or time specific, it may be taken as his limitation or his strength. But it is pretty clear that though a debut collection, it is definitely not a naïve experiment. His handling of language and particularly images is quite refreshing, and shows the potential of a mature poet. Nowhere does he follow any specific stanza pattern or any particular rhyme scheme. In fact, at one place he makes it clear, "freedom … that does not ponder/ how many words/must a poem/have to have/to be/a poem" ("Define Freedom"). His deliberate attempt to ignore the punctuation marks, make the poems open-ended. And still it's important to notice that the poem nowhere becomes vague or obscure. Though written in a free verse, one can easily experience musicality in it. A poem like "Morphine" lingers on the boundary of a lyric and a rap. Poems like "Some Days" and "Spaces" are indeed gems in this collection, which reveal Shrenik Jain's prospective as a promising poet. I am sure that the readers too will enjoy these poems and welcome Shrenik Jain's passionate venture.

- Dr. Nitin Jarandikar

Preface

If only I could write, the way I thought; these poems would be very different than what they are now. I don't know how they would fare, better or worse, but they would still be splinters from my mind, punched across these pages, under different names and themes.

Parts of these poems have been scribbled on my almirah, some lie in my cell phone, and most others have been written on the backs of various notebooks while my fingers were wet as I ran out of the bath, simply because I couldn't let a thought process escape my mind and my mouth after repeating a hundred times.

The only disadvantage I feel while presenting these poems is that they have been written on different subjects at different times under different circumstances and with different emotions, but they will be read all at once.

Bus journeys, isolation period during covid, hot baths, the time when my mind frisked away in between a conversation or an argument, moments while performing an examination on a patient, and other instances, have been a larger part of this collection.

Poetry has never found me any purpose, but it has burned an impression within me and I hope it brings you at the very least, an ember.

Acknowledgements

I would like to acknowledge the debt I owe to my parents, Dr. Shasmita Ravindra Jain and Dr. Ravindra Annappa Jain, who have always looked after me. My mother has been a cornerstone in my journey from a reader to a writer, having introduced me to the public library, at the age of seven years and gifting me with a membership at the same institution later. Without the support and care of my parents, I would not have been able to understand the world, the way I do now. I owe them more than an acknowledgement, but this should probably suffice for now.

Dr. Shreyans Ravindra Jain, my elder brother and a great friend, I thank you for putting up with me and taking all the heat for the problems I used to create as a younger sibling over all these years.

I would never have understood how editing was such a tedious and microscopic process that required laser-precision, if it wasn't for Dr. Nitin Jarandikar and Dr. Shubhangi Jarandikar. Their keen vision helped me discover how the absences of periods at the ends of sentences can change entire perspectives. In a very few words they led me to a different side of rewriting and visiting my work through reader's eyes.

I would like to thank my friends, Ashutosh Jarandikar and Ganesh Mardhekar for spending time in the making of this collection. If it hadn't been for their insight, their patience to bear with me and the midnight hunger-breaks this book would not have found its place here.

I would like to thank Shubhda Shinde, Pratiksha Punse and Riddhi Jadhav, for being great friends and always looking out for me during my time as a medical student among a crowd of strangers.

Kavita Thakur and Snehal Sawant, I give you my sincere thanks for always being there and providing me the courage to move ahead.

Ravindu Ghotavadekar and Anurag Gode, you guys have been the closest friends to me over these years and I cherish your friendship.

I remain forever indebted to the late Faeem Ansari, best friend and roommate, whose presence and laughter were probably the only things that I looked forward to everytime I retreated to my room. He stood for me in all of my difficulties, and became a cushion at my rock bottom. I owe you, Faeem, for your smiles and all the lessons you taught me. Your memories will pacify me, always.

1. Winter

it is winter
you arrive early
the cold has
started to set in
cutis that become ruins
of deserts that were once oasis
textures of alternates of
black over white over black
hair frail, mane thin
rooting from goosebumps
beneath lie the
powdery scales of
silver cleaved out
from bones
if only were they jewelry
but it burns the skin
in mornings under sun
the dermis in flames
winter's gift to my skeleton
are tattooed sins and
words that aren't names

winter demands
you nurture the corpus in
nan's oils, worn out hands
served their purpose
on nights such as these
you hibernate
when your warmth
longs for warmth
out of a fireplace
out of place
but cold creeps
into your sinuses
yet you still want
to hold your breath
through the night
just so that she can
sleep well, have a
morning that's right
and leave a trail
of footsteps in snow
a pattern in randomness
do you follow?

and if we ever falter
this winter love
that was
born in fall

bound to fail
let's never
look back
to this season
let's forget
this year and its
reasons
the bookmarked
Shakespeares
and half turned
Hemingways
just keep our
promises
that if we ever
lost our way home
remember
we are as much stars
as much stars are us

2. Some Days

some days you are lost
and i am the street
your fingers wander
tremble at turns
nescient of what
they might find
wounded corners
softer scars
giggles and squeals
of a girl chasing
dogs chasing cars

some days you are meadow
and i am the sheep
the sun is warm
on my skin
the sky is bleached
white fluff levitating
cotton grass
within my teeth
i bask in sunlight
siestas in the noon
you cradle and nourish

blood and belly
my rented soul
sacrificed by
the rising moon
some days we are nothing-
molecules of quiet
sharpening for tomorrow
miniscule our labours
our bodies
tied and tired
we burn for morrow
sweat and salt
we churn out
pebbles of chalk
the fire beside
lust-envies
thirst for
the fire inside

some days we are everything
everything of everything
intoxicated on grandiose
constellations sifting
within my fingers
and your hair
we make love
on a sky

drowned in blood
scrape paper skin
stars on napes
chase cracked voices
breaths running out
of breaths out of lungs
and cigarettes

3. H.e.r.

our first evening spent
is amongst crowds
walking-weaving
ankles brushing
fingertips kissing
finding familiarity
amidst our anxiety-
that swims in a sea of strangers
at our favourite coffee places
in the early dark
serving pancakes
and strawberry
flavored cliches

we revert to quarters
the ones we got after tea
rooms within rooms
the fourth floor
of a four storey building
the doors close behind
open in front of us
and she talks about
the dusk and the banality

of sunsets
i can't help but love her
yet not tell the first time
so i lean in and grab her ears
nobody has taught me to kiss
because such things
men don't discuss
eyes shut i pray
she closes hers as well
our puckered lips
form a vacuum and
swallow years off
of our time
in here we age too soon

the woke within me wakes
asks to ask for her 'sent
but the deed has been made
and the action been taken
my tongue rolling down hers
our lips sealed smitten
only moans escape
cutting the silence
of breaths that don't breathe
speak tongues i can't speak
though i wish i understood
latin and greek

not literally but
the underlying metaphors
how everything is sex
and how it isn't
i wish that i had been
a pirate in previous years
captaining distant seas
plundering shores
of different dialects
primate in habitat
with primal tongues
that hadn't tasted nothing;

our insecurities
strip in layers
form a heap
of dirty laundry
we steal glances
at each other's
naked selves
laughter escapes
in the atmosphere
and glimpses
turn into the intimacy
of forehead kisses

4. Not Too Long, Just Forever

darkness arrives untimely
with overcast and gloom
as we flop in the veranda
with her favourite novel
my head on her thighs
with an uncertain fate
that overhead looms

it feels like midnight
at seven in the evening
when lightning strikes
for a second
and restyles night into day
i see it stretch horizontally
from one end to the other
as it intermingles through
her fanned fingers facing the sky
lightning shreds itself into
a thousand parts
as time stretches along

i drown into a trance

of memories i wish i could re-live/relieve

like of the time
when she dropped her icecream
the first time we tried eating one
and ended up smearing it onto each other's faces- kissing
as earthquakes shuddered through our knees
and electricity through our veins

and

the first time i cried against her shoulders in a movie theatre
as the dusted heroes joined the surviving ones,
the second time
when a gauntlet donned iron-man
snapped his fingers together
her embrace consoled my weeping self

and

the first time she asked me
what my favourite colour was
and until then i hadn't one
so when she blurted 'lime'
i told her that she guessed right
ever since i haven't seen 'lime'
like before

i could die for it now
and

the first time we danced in rains
on her rooftop
i joked how her dress got to clung
to her skin and i couldn't
her smile burned through my paper heart;

so if she asks me now
of how much do i want
this second to last
i would say
'not too long, just forever'
and we would laugh at our cliche
romance
and go back to whatever

5. Bullets Fired During Peace

a stray bullet
hits me
in its path
i remember
the late dark
i washed my sins
in the river
that was once
jhelum in the north
waters lighter
than her ankles
on my shoulders
her name
singes the larynx
i radio
Romeo

the projectile
7.62 millimetres
lodged in guts
i have accumulated
broken skulls

for a country
i know nothing of
and people that
know nothing of me
India

i remember
sinatra on stereo
clothes in a pile
the peeled blankets
and the skin
we cast aside
i dissolved into her
we loved for
the lost time
and seas
that were free
beyond borders
wars fought
for soil
i guard my life
all the while
Delta

my body falls
knees capped
camouflaged torso

is crimson
i feel nothing
it feels good
to feel nothing
the Old Monk rum
within my blood
utters the synonyms
of existence
that's extinct-
battles in storms with
no compasses
no shelters
no homes
to gravitate
Delta

i remember
my mother
her palms
that weren't ready
to abandon my cheeks
her eyes were ocean
salt and forlorn heavy
father stood beside
forgetting the art
of embracing his child
his hand on mother's shoulder

strengthening her stride
i never looked back
until now
Hotel

and cheap rooms
i spent few minutes
talking to her
fabric slipped off
of our skeletons
the moment we enter
i was a brook
she the river
that was once jhelum
i flood into
my brain cells
are static
head bounces off
of my automatic
guns in the direction
of a landmine
dormant
on the borders of
India

6. Doxies

it is grey
raining outside
you sprawl against
my ribcage
breaths heavy
and whispers
that close silences
between us
your fingers scribble
sonnets on my
shoulders
the collar bone
a cistern of kisses
left behind
your lips solder
to my sternum
pour in poetry
lost in the echoes
my chest is a boombox
your tongue finds
its way into mine
mouths reach inside mouths
teeth click

laughter and
noses press together
eyes open into
souls
i absorb the scent
your hair
lilac and purple
scars that fit the
length of lips-
wounds, hollow pits
that exact the thumb
resting under the
blade of your scapulas
as i embrace the
warmth of your laughter
sunshine peeking over
my shoulders

we are reflections
in a window
of a man on his back and
a woman breaking against his pose
we are the thousand lovers
that have come before us
bolting from our tribes
where difference was a weapon
love could not shield

rains drip on the barks outside
that are witnesses to the
lovers past who have
tattooed into wood
scarred, engraved
stories with
endings, beginnings and middles
stories that weren't
stories to begin with
but letters, soft-worded whispers
that were breathed around
these birched skeletons
murals of lovers
-who transcended contradictions
- who are us

7. On Some days I'm a Volcano...

on days when it rains
and nights when it doesn't
i tattoo Van Gogh's sunflowers
at the root of my wrists
they remind me of empty spaces
that haven't been loved
that have been missed

on nights that are dark
and days that aren't
i read about poets and madmen
although there's not much difference
they remind me of myself
from a time
when i refused to leave
when i refused to love

on days when i am nothing
and nights when i'm more of the above
i feel like wanting to be a hurricane
far from better much towards worse
but sometimes i wish to be the sunshine

creep through cracked skies
to nourish, to nurse

and when all of it is smothering me
there's just one thing i need to ask of you
please don't look at me
like i need saving,
i know it
i do
instead just pretend and tell me that
'On some days I'm a Volcano
On others, The Earth'
that you won't let me break apart
that you will love me with warmth

8. The Phantom of Your Absence

like countless
other times
i find myself
under the warmth
inside a sweatshirt
that smells of you
a cocoon
of your arms
and i evolve

the white light
sprays itself
against the sky
in the mid of night
to its farthest limits
creeping through
burgundy curtains
ghosts of polyester
you have just ended
an hour long call to me
my breasts swim
in tides of your dreams

eyes stare into
the white and the black

the ruins of college-
buildings are silhouettes
phantoms in dark
the white is a blur
an ovoid lamp
an asterisk
through my spectacles
rays thrown
haphazard
a globe of
faint- aura
from the lamp
hangs by
loosely
woven threads
of a rainbow
a comet leaning
away from the moon
my mind is a kaleidoscope
and you keep
mirroring and multiplying

my daze breaks
i am brought to

this reality from another
an insidious change
in the breeze
chilly- stinging
the ghosts of these ruins
are haunted
by the darkness
crouching in my eyes
the white that entered
darkened the darkest
nights inside

i burn myself
you taught me how
a candle- a body
that melts
into wax and sweat
the scald of love
lost on romance
a wick that smoulders
doused on your nethers

9. Cigarettes that Kill

we make love on the window sill
wind in our hair
chafed bodies and
blood through our skin
with lips that sting
we surmise the part of me
the next cigarette kills

another one floats
through her lips
after sex
it tastes of charred rocks
i hope that is what my heart makes;
it's glowing end
dimly lights her facade
a tangerine glow and
ash that settle into the hollow
once the residence of my heart

having sent such many
tossing and twirling
through the window
to sink and swim

in the stinking gutter below
i light another one
send smoke the same way
to see if they still singe
to see if they still kill
another human perhaps
a part of her that still resides within

she chooses her sky and i choose mine
burn a hole in the blue vault
smoke upto three quarters of nine
butcher more kith and kin
another memory
the touch of her soft satin skin
poems that she backspaced
from her screen
the fuel within my lungs
the impel to not give in
everything i lose
i persuade myself
is a part of me the next cigarette kills

10. Buy Me A Heart

on fours i collect
frantically
for the pieces
of a heart
smashed broken
to put together
they cut
and cleave
laced with memories
of our love
that's venom
poison me
again
my nerves
they are prison

the pieces come together
the puzzle does not
a chunk lies missing
i search for it
a lost piece
of a treasure trove
flashlight on my forehead

lighthouse in a storm
my thoughts crash
and drown
in the sea
that is you
the heart was
a ship and it struck
an iceberg
lost its loot

i punch through
my stabbing-
aching chest
the ribcage
flaps underwater
inside a shard
clings onto me
rakes the lungs
protruding from spaces
between curved bones
it hurts
a thousand hells
i don't know
how hell hurts
probably
a thousand

fucking-fucks

i am on fours
retching-dying
realising
a part of you
will kill me again
but living is
delaying death
and for that
i need another
heart in my chest

11. Acacia

you run
along the cracks
in my skin
the veins
are streets
for your feet
to bleed in
your voice
chases corners
like widows
their phantom
sons and daughters
you've poured
into me
wine in goblets
marrow in bones
dissolved into
iota and atoms
become every bit
of flesh and morsel
you are acacia nilotica
in my iron lungs
thorns pressing from within

bullet holes in bronchioles
i plunge my hand
into my mouth
retch as fingertips
screech the bark
that hangs behind
and uproot the acacia-
the snowstorm in my breast
with the pedicle in my fist
i pull out the tree like
a cork from a flagon
my elbow gashes against
overhanging incisors
the roots root out
parasites in my soul
everything bleeds
from inside and
i want to drown
as much as
hurt may allow
torment to thicken
and replace the air
with stagnant vacance-y
that reverberates
with the world
i cannot be a part of
the music that emanates

from strings- alloy,
the smell of nickel
rusting against my
clavicle on tears
and salt that
eats away from the nucleus
a rat nibbling at a cheese deck
holes on a screen i can't paint
the music is inaudible-
illegible notes on a paper
i don't remember
a time that you
weren't here
i don't know
what i am
going to do
without you
inside me

12. Contraband

and i cross the street
ruminating how
my fingers had gotten used to
holding yours
the pearl ring
encircling
your left index finger
i clutched like a trigger
every street i cross now
i hold your memory
like a prayer
on my fingers and lips

i think back to
how in quarantine
we used to steal
bits and bits
to put together
from a time
that was stashed
contraband
and years later
of what was left-

a rubber band
stretched
and stretched
until we had
no more of it
to break off
at one end
we would split
still doing things
still smoking
in the reminiscence
of a negotiated end

i recall
how the car stopped upon
seeing our hands
in its yellow lights
allowing us for a
crossing- the last crosses on a
march summer night
slipping pinstripes
of black and white
for colors had started to vanish
from our fading fingers
and before i felt the tears
stream down
my cheeks were thin

and air was what
left of us

so we blew
on different paths
on different journeys
hoping to materialize
at a crossroads
in black and white
and paint our souls
the color at the back
of another, color
wrung inside out
from a sleepless dream
where the night never ended
and the sun was never found

13. Blue

i inch towards the precipice
an edge of the roof
in front of me
and i feel closer to gravity
more than ever
with every step
i find myself free
the nicotine stick slips
drowns into thin air
before plunging onto
the ground below
somewhere
mid-air
the burnt end glows brighter
breaking oxygen molecules
faster than ever
the red and orange
fades into ash and black
it's existence now complete
the earth finds its carbon back
death looks inviting
clearly feels enticing
to burn mid life

find our purpose
leave no trace
no stain, no corpus
they have held me
for a while now
these blue skies
tomorrow they will
find me.
find me purple
and turquoise.

14. Define Freedom

you tell me
freedom is
to be
a poem
immune from its
structure
seagulls
in the breeze
buoyant on
salty waters
only I have been
caged my entire
life that has forgotten
what it is to fly
wings that don't
remember-you
mistake paper
for skin
that's yellow
i ask you to
riddle me with lead
periods
at the ends of these

sentences.
bullet holes
at the end of this life
sentenced by judges
who break gavels
instead of nibs
you tell me
what freedom is
you bind it
in a bracket
of what you
mean it to be
its further than far
as the eyes can see
it is the feather
lost at sea
a breeze astray
in canyons and valleys
it is a revolutionary
in black waters
it is the countless lives
martyred
against fourth dimension
devoid of time
and history
that does not ponder
how many words

must a poem
have to have
to be
a poem

15. Step Into Nothingness

i have been locked
in a room colossal
white enough
to blind a sane man
but i am not (the former)

the walls run for miles
the ceiling an inch
higher than sky
the floor is ivory
the air reeks iron
suffocating

you would think my voice
would carry and echo
but there isn't one sound
not even my own
for it does not leave me;
my larynx is paper
crushed by the man
who locked me

i am raged

i am terrified
this ordeal
seems futile
to find myself
i was supposed
to lose first.

lose to whom?
lose myself where?
lose at what?

these walls of woe
encroaching upon me
or to
this ceiling of void
threatening to
crash down on me
or maybe
this reflection
that has been staring
ever since the door
behind, was closed on me

the air is vacuum
thinner than it was before
it's clear what need be done
of what i have to lose

just life another breath
this reflection of mine
i strangulate
i lock myself behind
step into nothingness

16. The Alphabet Song of Suicide

across nights i lie
by myself outside of my body
carving into the spine to see if i feel
discounting the will to
euthanize, to see me
fall from my eyes onto a
gleaming dagger that flirts to commit
harakiri but i am drowning in debt
incurred by life
just in case death was fair and
kind enough to
let me know
my time had reached the last swing
notice my
obsession of arranging and rearranging this
poem around my neck
quick to tightening
rate my expiration out of ten
seven atleast i
tried my best
until i couldn't-anymore feel my
veins keeping me from

words that would choke me to the
xiphisternum puffed against a
yawn that is more of a
zombie's maw

17. Unfinished

an unfinished poem
awaits me
within the pages of
my forgotten diary
worn-out- torn
debilitated
a sonnet fragmentary
rather expurgated

in a world of crippled lovers
and teenagers pulverized
lie dreams fractured
and their severed benevolence

of incomplete verses
and ballads unsung
leaflets shredded with
words unwritten

of commas or
colons

the periods and
exclamations
dashes or hyphens
apostrophes and quotations
are we even asking the right questions?
of muffled screams
and drowned anguish
borrowed breaths
and stories unconcluded
of dying hopes
and mirrored obscurity
a million poets
and miserly poetry

18. Morphine

your eyes tell you
are being injected happiness
through an iv line
an ampoule
breaking against
forceps that hold
your depression still
for your brain is running
out of serotonin
and grief
runs within
ventricles like
worms squirming
in wormholes
pain everywhere
every where they haven't touched
is a place where your skin isn't sin_
full of dopamine
decreasing
desecrating the sanctity
of your brain
that is the desolate
ruins of a medieval castle

a labyrinth of rooms
abandoned
happiness was once lightning
through your blood
that seeped in the sponge
of the skin and c(o)ursed;
now there's no electricity
but a thunderclap uprising
a temporal stream
gushing, flooding
the walls of skull
dams breaching.
Ever feel so much
That it is noxious
To the prescription pills?
that tumble from a hidden
corner in your almirah
and you fumble to hide them
because you can't
hide behind them
and anxiety is the diagnosis
that makes you want to
tear off the scabs on
the wounds that have just
stopped bleeding
that makes you want to erode
and pick

and pick
and pick
until you reach the bone where
pain has a latency (to kill)
so you pile-up
the fragments of
dermis debris
and put them together
jigsaw on your wounds
you take one and
attach
attach
attach
attack
the anxiety who debates
if you are worthy of happiness
of the endorphins
gamma, alpha, beta
swimmers in a race
to the finish line of
perception where the prize
is a state of euphoria
too much of laughter is a poison
but you don't care
for opium and endorphins
are chemically similar
and when they are upstream

you can smile
and have sex
like a machine
newly installed
into work
- penis inside a vagina
- penis inside a vagina
- penis inside the vagina
- penis inside the vagina
- penis inside her vagina
- penis inside her vagina
- penis in your fist
and you run out of endorphins
that are high when you
eat your favorite meals
but recently
you haven't
and happiness
is subjective
morphine isn't
so you don't want to feel
and feel the fake chuckling
you'd rather OD
and feel the gripping
of pain that
does not discriminate
between strays and society

arrives fashionably late
hours, at times days
oh wait there's pain
there's pain
hi there pain
here's ibuprofen
pills to swallow
whole without water
just don't cut your throat
your therapist advises
you should name
your anxiety
your anxiety
yours?
anxiety. it's just there.
do you have anxiety?
why?
what do you name it?
anxiety? he? she? it?
you now have another reason to be anxiously anxious
about naming your anxiety

19. I am Not

I feel like a spoon
In the bowl that was empty before
Isolated and oblique
It could have lay with the other spoons
In the mahogany mug on the third shelf but
It is here-lying
Isolated and oblique
I can't hold my head
In my thighs for longer
I have teeth that are tombstones
Imbued on my graveyard skin
I can't stay between my elbows where-
In lay the alcohol stained kisses
Indicating towards the signs on my
Icarus wings, that have dropped
In the streets of jericho
I tell you
I'm afraid when
I don't know what
I am afraid of
I flap away the
Irritating mosquito by my ear
I slap myself a hundred times

In my mirror
I am ugly
I tell my
Image
"
I hope your breath
Is the
Illusion that keeps me alive.
It is the air I believe You
Inhale and keep my lungs afloat.
"
I believe things to be true (or untrue)
Immune to the belief that hope
Is brighter than truth
I believe you when you talk about the
Isles of glass left in the mirror frame
I believe you when you tell me
I will survive
In this purgatory
In another life
I will find an escape
I am the end of my suffering

20. Sayan

when you were a boy
in summer
with a body
that fit in between
the two walls of a balcony
you used to lay down
a mattress of wool
rest your back on
one wall and
fold a mat of grass
around yourself
wall all around your body
except for the top
from where you allowed
this contraption
to let sunlight in
you shut your mortal
inside reading
bond and narayan
lost your ears to
presley and rahman
watching phosphenes
only leaving for lunches

the uncapped-canopy
was your knowledge-bubble
a cubicle you built
in an alley
of walls that were home
Summer ended
when August soil
welcomed petrichor
and you were back
to Shalom International School
on Chesson road
you missed an assembly
with two other girls
and were left in
an empty classroom
scribbling on the board
when the girls asked
you to erase
the sunlight and phosphenes
from the board that was your summer
you did not
the next day when you arrived
you felt cold shoulders
poking your ribs
every fair child in the room
staring at your skin
you set down your bag

where Miss Vandana
used to stick notes
of grades and scores
your name at the top
of all of them
you at the bottom
of the classroom crew
the board compared
it's color to that of your skin
and caste whose name
was probably a sin
and your hand me downs
that shouldn't have been handed
by nobody
an entire flock laughed
as you bawled
chasing tears
to the restroom
where the mirror
was your only friend
who did not ridicule

you thought about the words
shakespeare wrote into
how it had defined centuries
of literature and history
tagore's manasi

premchand's short stories
wrote themselves on the mirror
in clearing condensation
you thought about tupac shakur's
rhymes and gangsta signs
how his genius was alive
even after years-twenty five
van gogh's asylum
where his calm found canvas
oils and turpentine on brushes
that lathered, mixed
different forms of painting
different styles of the same art
you also thought
of the words and spiel
they couldn't
paper down
their contemplations- goliath
that ran frantic in their minds-
static as their fingers got to toil
everything they had to say
and the potential to say more
they all had their stories
you had not the courage
i had not the apology

summer was far away

you only had to
lid your cubicle

i am sorry

21. Not Here

i am home
and you're still
standing in front
of the mirror in
another dimension
with your penis
hanging
a wick about to burn
inside of a chest
that feels like
a battle raged snow globe
you are sweating
fear and sorrow
collapsing
no bones to hold
the sunken in your
eyes that are sinkholes
portals to different times-
blackholes
where the past slips past
the memories of our time
when we were one but
nowhere to hide

when was the last i slept?
when was the last that i was you?
was it then in the basement
when beside you
lay a gun
you used
to fuse
the joints of your chest
soldered just in case
your ribs chose to explode
confetti and blood

tick-tick-tick-tick
the ejection click
of nitroglycerine
through the ventricles
and vessels
of a heart
strapped with dynamite
a never ending code
being dialed into
a button pad
numbers and figures
i can't find any letters
to fill your larynx
but i should be able
to find you a song

or sounds of
the crackle of bacon
and sternum
the hendrix guitar
a silent hum
of lies between
your skin and flesh
the steps of our time
tattooed in morse
playing hide and seek;
the spirit has left
from your soul and
i am the fire brigade
that waters trees

Tell me.
Where's my out?

22. Maslow's Pyramid

the hierarchy of needs
considers love and belonging
at the third level,
neither at the top
nor at the bottom

the most human(e) needs
make up the foundation
while the desire to become
the most one can be,
spikes the top

self esteem and security
make up for the vacant levels in between
nevertheless one can only wonder
if all our needs
need be structured
under a pyramid
with one pecking order over the other;
if everything that mattered
to be human
was just another perfect little mould
and not be amoeboid

a never ending state
an infinitude

to be human
is to lose yourself in a labyrinth
with no exit
having had no entrance

to be human
is to strive, and fall
pick yourself up
pat your back
and get going

to be human
is to survive with/out
is to feed on concrete
and make the most of it

but to be, this human!
a paper being-
closing in on fire
requires passion
a certain drive-
that sets your heart pounding
like a F1 car with Hamilton in the seat;
it's love that's fuel

it's love that burns and 'burns'

so when i say that
we are all shit at being humans
i mean to tell you
that we are shit
according to Maslow's hierarchy
and that Maslow too
was just another person,
one of us
so pyramid or no pyramid
or whatever baseless
structureless form
a human's needs may take
Dear Maslow, it's love at the core
it always is love
always will be

23. The Window

the window
is
a slit in the wall
a slut in its character
emanates secrets
to neighbours such
laundered talks
races and politics
money and affairs
people and public

is built
not hollowed
out from a wall
not a cavity
worn into a bailey
with frames
glass panes
half open
open-complete
such its function
to look upon

humdrum
chaos and
commotion

the windows
inside
watch men
burn cigarettes
on their wives' skin
outside
look away
from men
malign
at women smoking

the windows
and their edges
their ledges
onto them
etched
lovers lullabies
scraped with
bare nails
rust and tears
the wood
and iron rails
paper planes

flutter in the wind
dreams, passengers
on there plummet
dying instead.
widows in valleys
artists and leaves/lives
pages uninked
swarm-dust
ash and singe

24. Melancholy Now

your tongue is sandpaper
on my tongue,
that was a rusting anchor
drowning in saltwater;
my mandible was in shackles.
no other word makes my mouth
as tender as your name
that hooks onto
my wallpaper heart
and scrapes the cardium
and it's wounds
like paint that sticks
underneath my fingernails
when i tear into the sky.
i remember whispering
the words to my favourite song
and my class teacher
asking me, if i was okay.
so i weaved silences large enough
to run away
from conversations
that felt like timer strapped
bombs on the sun

i loved reading
and holding a page
reading,
re-reading
the same words
until they meant more than they meant,
but i was afraid
that my tongue would ruin
the words
the same way,
my sweat worn fingers
would destroy the page.
i am now terrified
of everything that is happening,
your tongue is a language
i have never known,
yet i am still learning to love
and still learning to love you
but the songs and poems
of the past are half
of my half life.
so i write melancholy;
so i write in the past tense.

25. World War Next

i wonder if
roses would turn to rust
of a muzzle

on a gun
unfired dead between our fingers
in the war

fought with atoms
i wish to be born
a higgs boson

life might have
some mass after all if
not mine.

at post apocalypse
time would no longer be
a paradigm there

won't exist the
need to smooch our lips
for you and

i will be
stellar burst of red giants
across the system
in absolute chaos
our bodies would be memorials
of the battles

we fought everyday
the scars- medallions on breasts
to boast to

our grandchildren who
will figure out their own
wars to war

once they accept
that we are all dead
living tombstones looking

to disappear in
concrete and the hard floor
having had no

goodbyes or farewells
we were vikings dead floating
across the streams

at world's end
floating towards the steeper chasm
no flaming arrows

flying to set
us burning and give ends
to our stories

that began with
atoms and roses before wars
to never perish

26. R. V. Human

at the peak of civilization
the helm of everything
society breaks
its shackles
we find that
unchained hands
were never worthy
of freedom
dystopia-
bureaucrat
corporate
democrat
incinerates
a generation
that seeks
escape from reality
not that the world
already doesn't;
and men that don't know
how to hug
their fathers
preach about
the phoenix

tired of rising
from its ashes
life-after-life
postponing death
weddings expire-
drugs and contract papers
people say
i love you
while their mobile
screens display
appointments for
sex in the afternoons
children of men
sit atop
mountains of
debts and interests
compounding
people dying
in numbers-
figures
on television
screens
people running
our countries
the world
wear skeletons
like clothes

swaps faces
for masks
and everything sells
for a right price-
a right answer
from crayons
to chaos
and violence
under the banner
of righteousness
guns on hire
books are banned
poems are burned
on pedestals of your
favourite candles
ash rises through cities
of the dead in graves
rallying in streets
for their rights
to stay dead
mortified people
no race
no creed
human?
not so much

27. Faeem

it is cold
the fires have died
people retreat
into their homes
behind doors
but you are still
outside and numbing
you put on
an oversized jacket
the one he left behind
enter the room
behind a wall
pistachio and yellow
a vinyl of a tree
and birds free
a half done art
a tyre-less bike
and you want to feel
him and his laughter
that still rings
in the corridor
after his demise
he's not gone

you say
he'll be back
for his hoodie
and the harley dream
if only his lungs
hadn't given up
their only function
of breathing
you would be
on the top of leh
with him and your bikes
shuddering
if only he hadn't died
the night you returned
from speaking to him
for the last
his words to you
'i will be back soon'
if only he hadn't

but he didn't just die then
he dies everyday
every time
you enter the room
behind the wall
you switch on
the shared lamp

after night falls
you think
of quitting smoking
before lighting another
you laugh at his laugh
on a mobile screen wallpaper
youtube hosts kishore kumar
and his songs on loop
he dies everyday
until you put him to sleep
yourself for the last time
the tyre on the bike
the cigarettes crushed in thrash
accepting the corridors won't sing
and you are waving to him
outside of your room
slow and heavy
you wave until
your arms ache
time is a suspension
between you and him
it always was
a finger width
it only gets colder
from here
but you have
his oversized jacket.

28. I am everything that I was supposed to be

i write into my mother's handwriting-
strewn across the pages of a forgotten diary
she talks through her college days,
rants about her professors
and their condescension,
how women could never make
good doctors and how she decided
to prove them all wrong.
she writes fast, abrupt but
with surgical precision,
the errors err out of fullscape
and yet she writes soft-
a lullaby on papyrus
uninterrupted and immersive-
dolphins in a distant dream.
i write into her letters-
cursive that don't break
a sweat
and commas that don't break
sentences.
i write into her words
like climbing onto her shoulders

and gripping tight across her chest,
as she carries my tired self
from a sunday afternoon market.
i trace my path across the curves
of every syllable, that are keys
on a cartograph, and i am the
dot on a GPS map
walking into her footsteps,
across the porcelain pavements-
gliding, guided by mother's
handwriting
and i will continue to do so
until i am able of writing
my own story on the foundation
of my mother's words that
are testament.

29. Spaces

that person has left a void,
a blank space/ an empty tabloid
and i want to fill/and cram/ this void with anything? i can find
so i write/and stitch-these-words/and bind
hoping that these words fill up the empty spaces
hoping that these words willgetsuckedup into the vacuum
that keeps staring at me from places
but there are still those spaces /in between
w o r d s that terrify me
spaces /in between
w o r d s that mortify me
keep reminding me of the

emptiness

.

so I try to /write in betweenthemtoo.

andthennothingmakessense
nothingmakessenseatall

itisallacrapballoflettersandwordsthatdon'tmeanathing
butiunderstandthat
spaces are important
spaces are vital
spaces are significant
for things to make sense
for us to rant out/wipe our ledgers/
for us to grow;
grow into those spaces
grow up /and at times
grow a p a r t .

people will always fill/feel emptiness
temporarily,
and then they will leave or
perhaps we will
but this leaving and filling of spaces and voids and gaps and draughts
will keep us wanting/always and for more.

sometimes filling up these empty spaces
will suffocate you/clog you/drown you
in the same boat with a sinkhole under your feet.

you will leave and you will leave/live a void

9 798886 849431

Printed by Libri Plureos GmbH in Hamburg, Germany